Journey into the Bible

Lois Rock

Andrew Rowland

LION
CHILDREN'S

Contents

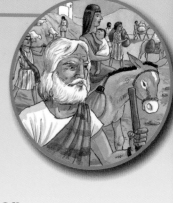

Route plan

This book will take you on a journey through time. It is your chance to visit some of the most important scenes from Bible times. The stories of the Bible are between 2,000 and 3,000 years old.

Why go there?

The Bible is one of the most important books in the history of the world.

The older part contains the holy books, or scriptures, of the Jews. The newer part consists of writings about Jesus that are special to Christians. They call these writings the New Testament and the Jewish scriptures the Old Testament.

Useful languages

Old Testament

Most of the stories were written in Hebrew, the language of the Jewish people. The stories of Daniel, set in Babylon and Persia, were written in Aramaic.

New Testament

Aramaic was the language that Jesus spoke. However, the books about him were written in Greek – a language understood far and wide in his day.

Nowadays, the Bible has been translated into many modern languages. You can journey into the Bible in English.

Some words to know

Shalom (Hebrew): an everyday greeting meaning "peace".
Abba (Aramaic): "daddy".
Christ (Greek): "chosen king".

Beginning the journey

The Bible stories take place in the lands on the eastern shores of the Mediterranean Sea. At the centre is a curving strip of land watered by great rivers. It was a good place to grow crops. There was also grass for sheep, goats, and cattle. This fertile crescent is the setting of the oldest stories in the Bible.

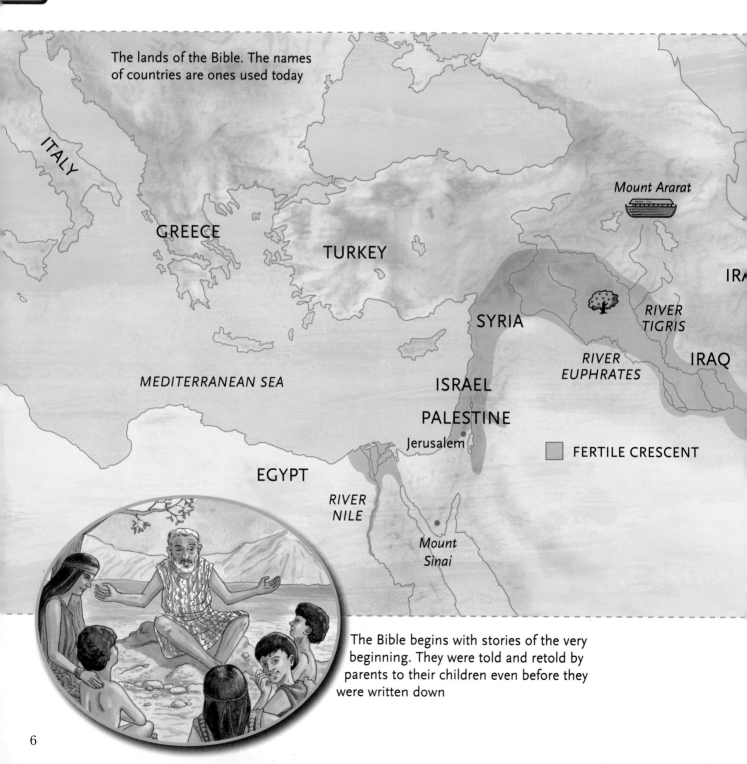

The lands of the Bible. The names of countries are ones used today

ITALY

GREECE

TURKEY

Mount Ararat

SYRIA

RIVER TIGRIS

RIVER EUPHRATES

IRAQ

IRA

MEDITERRANEAN SEA

ISRAEL

PALESTINE

Jerusalem

FERTILE CRESCENT

EGYPT

RIVER NILE

Mount Sinai

The Bible begins with stories of the very beginning. They were told and retold by parents to their children even before they were written down

The garden of Eden

The Bible stories of creation say that, in the beginning, God planted a garden in Eden. It was watered by four rivers, including the River Tigris and the River Euphrates. The garden was a paradise home for the first man, Adam, and the first woman, Eve. The wicked serpent tempted Adam and Eve to eat forbidden fruit. When they did, they let all manner of evil things into the world.

Noah's ark

The Bible story of Noah is about a great flood. God wanted to wash away the world's wickedness and make a new start. God found one good man, Noah, and told him to build a huge boat to save the animals. After the flood, so the story goes, the ark grounded on Mount Ararat.

Travel tip

The lands of the Bible mostly have hot, dry summers. The winters are cooler, and it is then that most rain falls. Major floods are rare, but heavy rainstorms can cause "flash floods" when rivers overflow.

Winter snow is possible on higher ground. Mount Ararat is high enough to be snow-capped all year round.

The Abraham trek

The Bible story of the people of Israel really begins with Abraham. Abraham's journey began in the city of Ur. His father, Terah, took the family to Haran. When Abraham was a grown man, he believed God was calling him to go to Canaan and make it his home.

Haran

MEDITERRANEAN SEA

CANAAN

EGYPT

Ur

This map shows Abraham's route from his first home to Canaan

Abraham needed to be able to go from place to place to find pasture for his animals. He and his family lived in tents

Servants dig a well

Servants cook

Girls weave cloth

On the move

In Canaan, Abraham lived the life of a nomad with his family and his flocks. When the rains failed and there was little for people or animals to eat, Abraham journeyed on to Egypt. He later returned and became wealthy: he had flocks and cattle as well as silver and gold.

The promise

God promised Abraham that he would be the father of a great nation. They would be God's special people and they would bring God's blessing to all the world.

Travel tip

Anyone doing the Abraham trek is expected to walk. Sandals or leather boots are suitable. At times the journey will be along a well-used trading route. Other times you will go off to rough pastures.

Heavy baggage will be carried by donkeys. There will be an ox cart at all times if you get tired and need to ride for part of the trip.

Servants and their families

Boys learn to hunt with bows and arrows

Abraham

Sarah and Isaac

Children help mind the flocks

Corn in Egypt

A great river runs through Egypt: the River Nile. Each year the river flooded, leaving moist, fertile soil on the fields. The Egyptians had good harvests and became wealthy. They had wonderful buildings filled with treasures. This is the setting of the Bible story of Joseph.

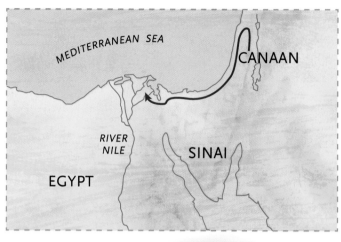

Joseph's journey to Egypt

Joseph

Joseph was a proud young man. He was proud to know he was a great-grandson of Abraham. He was even prouder to know that he was the favourite son of his father, Jacob.

Jacob – also known as Israel – had twelve sons. Ten of them were older than Joseph. Even so, it was to Joseph that Jacob gave an expensive cloak. This gift showed that Joseph was the chosen heir.

Joseph boasted about dreams he had in which his mother, father, and brothers all bowed down to him.

His boasting made his brothers hate him. One day they beat him up and sold him to slave traders. He was bought as a slave in Egypt. Little by little, he earned respect for his hard work and loyalty. More than that, he could explain dreams. He believed it was God who helped him to do so.

Travel tip

Purple dye for cloth is a speciality of Canaan. It is made from a type of shellfish found on its seashore. In fact, Canaan is sometimes called "the land of purple". Purple-dyed cloth is very expensive, but a great souvenir.

Joseph's wonderful coat of red, blue, and purple

A slave market in Egypt

One day, he explained the king's dreams to him. They foretold years of bad harvests ahead. Joseph was put in charge of storing grain from the good harvests to last through the years of bad harvests.

In the end, Joseph's brothers came from Canaan. They were starving and begged to buy grain. They had no idea that the man with whom they were pleading was their brother. When Joseph saw they were sorry for what they had done, he told them who he was. He asked all his family to come to Egypt.

"It was really God who sent me to Egypt," he explained. "God wanted me to be able to help you now."

The grain harvesting in a good year in Egypt

Irrigation shaduf

Harvesting with sickle

Storing

Joseph

Slaves building grain silos

Sinai

The wilderness named Sinai lies between Egypt and Canaan. It is a dry and dusty place with scraggy plants and rocky hills. One of these hills is called Mount Sinai. It is famous as the place where God spoke to a prophet named Moses.

The people spent forty years in the wilderness of Sinai

Slaves in Egypt

From the time of Joseph, Jacob's sons and their entire families lived in Egypt. They were sometimes called the Hebrews, but they thought of themselves as Jacob's people – or, to use Jacob's other name, the people of Israel.

Years passed, and there was one king after another. Then came a king who was fearful of having so many foreigners in his land. He made the people of Israel his slaves and treated them harshly. They had to make bricks for the splendid new cities he wanted.

Moses and the great escape

God chose a man named Moses to rescue them and take them back to Canaan. This was to be their new home. On the way, God spoke to Moses.

God gave the people laws: about loving God and one another.

Turban

Menorah

High priest

Breastplate with twelve jewels

Incense altar

Table for offerings of bread

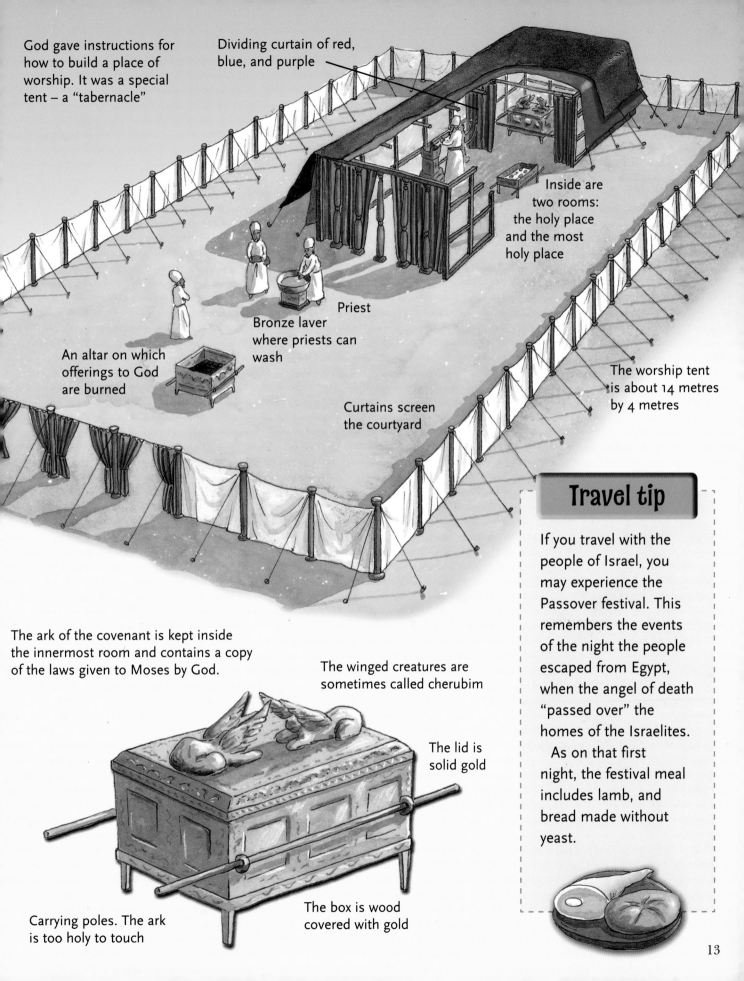

God gave instructions for how to build a place of worship. It was a special tent – a "tabernacle"

Dividing curtain of red, blue, and purple

Inside are two rooms: the holy place and the most holy place

Priest

Bronze laver where priests can wash

An altar on which offerings to God are burned

The worship tent is about 14 metres by 4 metres

Curtains screen the courtyard

The ark of the covenant is kept inside the innermost room and contains a copy of the laws given to Moses by God.

The winged creatures are sometimes called cherubim

The lid is solid gold

Carrying poles. The ark is too holy to touch

The box is wood covered with gold

Travel tip

If you travel with the people of Israel, you may experience the Passover festival. This remembers the events of the night the people escaped from Egypt, when the angel of death "passed over" the homes of the Israelites. As on that first night, the festival meal includes lamb, and bread made without yeast.

13

Down on the farm in Canaan

Visit a farm in Canaan at any time of year and you will find plenty going on.

Joshua

After many years in the wilderness, Moses led his people to the edge of Canaan. He did not live to enter the land and Joshua became the new leader.

The Canaanites did not want to make room for the people of Israel. The first obstacle Joshua faced was the walled city of Jericho. He believed God told him what to do: he ordered the people of Israel to get ready for battle and march around the city every day for seven days. Then, when they blew the trumpets and shouted aloud, the walls fell down.

This miracle convinced everyone that God wanted the people of Israel to settle the land. Little by little, they made it their home.

Joshua's motto

When he was old and the land was won, Joshua called the people together. "You must make a choice," he said, "about whom you will worship. As for me and my house, we will serve the Lord, our God." Everyone agreed to do the same.

Joshua settled the land of Canaan

MEDITERRANEAN SEA

CANAAN

Jericho

DEAD SEA

Goats

Bedrooms

The roof space is a place to work and to relax

Grinding grain with a quern

A pillared house

The lower floor is for animals

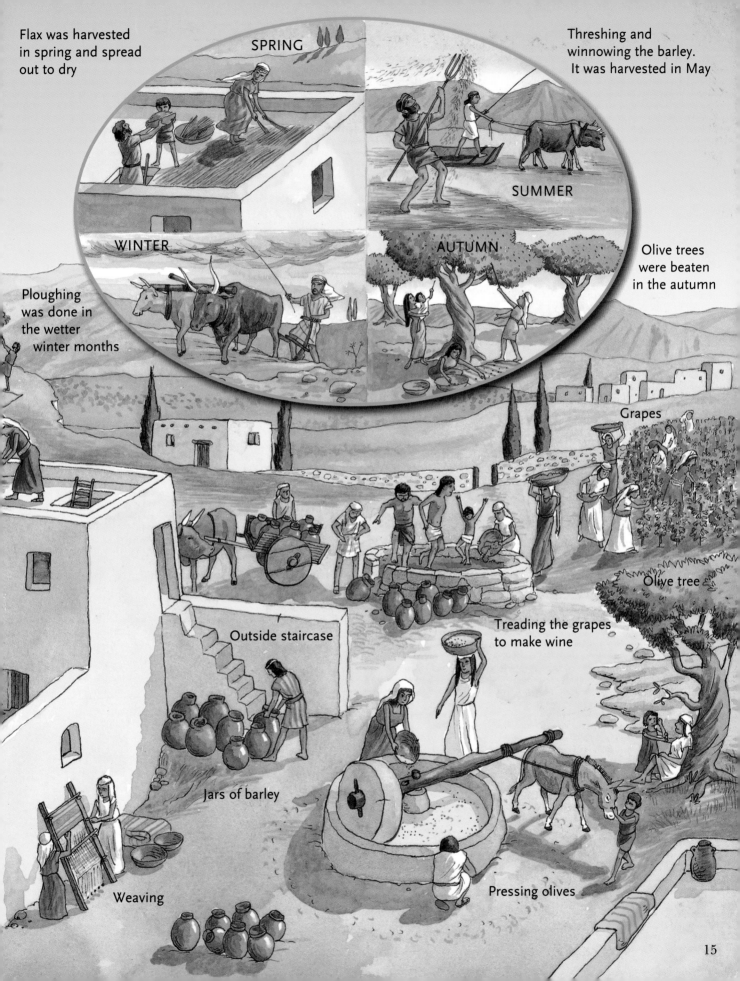

Flax was harvested in spring and spread out to dry

SPRING

Threshing and winnowing the barley. It was harvested in May

SUMMER

WINTER

AUTUMN

Ploughing was done in the wetter winter months

Olive trees were beaten in the autumn

Grapes

Olive tree

Outside staircase

Treading the grapes to make wine

Jars of barley

Weaving

Pressing olives

A Philistine city

When the people of Israel settled Canaan, they faced many enemies. The most troublesome were the Philistines. These people had arrived by sea from Crete many hundreds of years before. The Egyptians had fought them off their land, so they moved along the coast towards Canaan. There they built five cities.

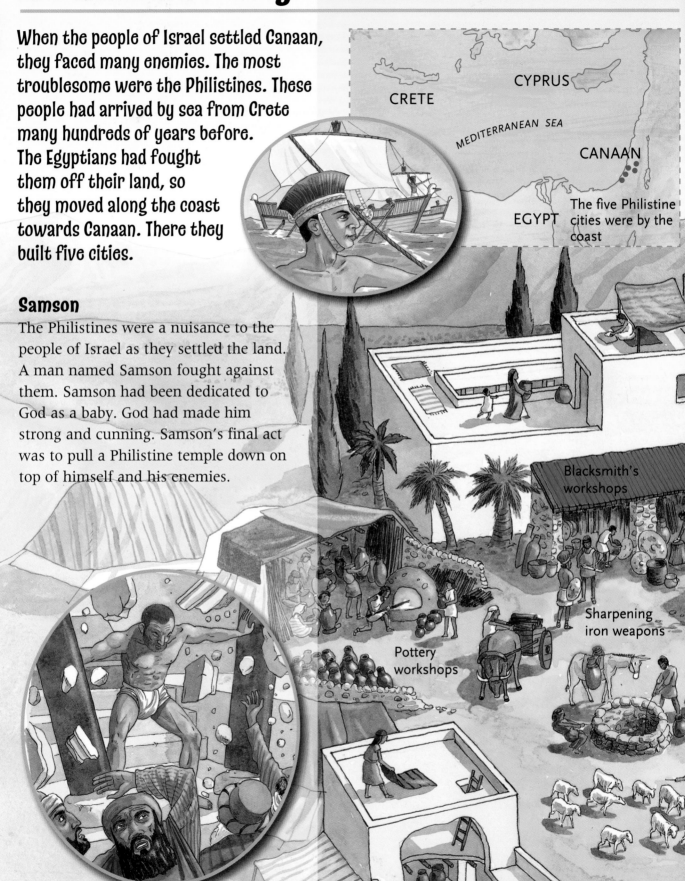

The five Philistine cities were by the coast

Samson

The Philistines were a nuisance to the people of Israel as they settled the land. A man named Samson fought against them. Samson had been dedicated to God as a baby. God had made him strong and cunning. Samson's final act was to pull a Philistine temple down on top of himself and his enemies.

Blacksmith's workshops

Sharpening iron weapons

Pottery workshops

David

Years passed, but the Philistines never gave up fighting the people of Israel. Once they even captured the ark of the covenant. They only sent it back because they suffered some kind of disaster wherever it went.

One day, the Philistine army and the Israelite army were camped opposite each other. The Philistines sent a champion out: the giant Goliath. He had sharp iron weapons and strong armour.

"If one of you Israelites can beat me, you win the battle," he cried.

Brave David was a shepherd boy who was visiting his soldier brothers. His only weapon was a sling for throwing stones.

But he cried, "I fight you in the name of my God."

David knocked Goliath down and won.

emple for
e worship
the Philistine
od Dagon

Travel tip

Philistine pottery is very special and worth looking out for. The designs are a lot like those seen on ancient pottery from Crete – which is where the Philistines first came from. A jar with a fish design is a good reminder of these "Sea People".

The capital: Jerusalem

David is famous for defeating the Philistine Goliath. In fact, he defeated all his nation's enemies. When he became king, he chose a city to be the capital of his kingdom: Jerusalem.

Underground attack

David had to capture the place he wanted for his city. It was a hilltop fort that belonged to the Jebusites. The steep hillside made it difficult to attack. David and his men knew a secret: there was a tunnel from outside the city that linked to a well inside the city. The soldiers crawled along the tunnel and made a surprise attack.

MEDITERRANEAN SEA

CANAAN

Jerusalem was the site of David's city

Shiloh

Jerusalem

DEAD SEA

David wanted Jerusalem to be the place where people would worship God. Since the time his people had entered Canaan, the ark of the covenant had stayed in the tabernacle, which stood at a place called Shiloh. David had it brought to Jerusalem.

God chose David's son Solomon to build the Temple itself.

Royal palace

Temple built by
Solomon

City wall

Solomon looks at
plans for the Temple

City gate

Travel tip

You can expect to
see some spectacular
Temple processions in
Jerusalem. The music
is loud and lively, and
the crowds often dance
alongside the dancers
in the procession.

19

The Assyrian enemy

After Solomon's time, his kingdom was divided into two: Israel and Judah. For many years, both kingdoms struggled to fight off their enemies. Then came the most terrifying enemy of all: Assyria. Their army was the most feared in all the world.

The extent of the Assyrian empire

Attack

Emperor Sennacherib of Assyria was confident. The kingdom of Israel was already defeated. He had already captured some of Judah's walled cities. The biggest prize lay before him: Jerusalem.

Inside Jerusalem's walls, King Hezekiah of Judah was saying his prayers. The Assyrian army was camped all around. He knew his people were trapped. Only God could save them.

Then something amazing happened. Overnight, many thousands of Assyrian soldiers died. Emperor Sennacherib led his army away. Surely it was a miracle.

Jonah

The story of Jonah is set in the time of the Assyrians, in their capital city of Nineveh.

The story has a surprising message: God does not want to punish the Assyrians; rather, God wants them to mend their ways. So the prophet Jonah is asked to warn them. Instead, he tries to run away by sailing from Joppa to Tarshish, the country on the western shores of the sea now known as the Mediterranean.

A whale swallows him and brings him back to shore. Then he goes and preaches to the king and the people. To his amazement, they are sorry for their wrongdoing. And God forgives them.

Messengers from Hezekiah plead with the Assyrians

Captives are led away

Travel tip

Learn from the story of Jonah and beware of taking sea trips without checking the weather! Storms on the great sea, now called the Mediterranean, can be severe.

By the rivers of Babylon

Babylon was the city at the heart of a huge empire. Its armies defeated the Assyrians and their lands. In the year 597 BCE, King Nebuchadnezzar II of Babylon took Jerusalem. Ten years later, he destroyed the city and its Temple and took many of the people of Judah to live in Babylon. The people of Judah became known as the Jews.

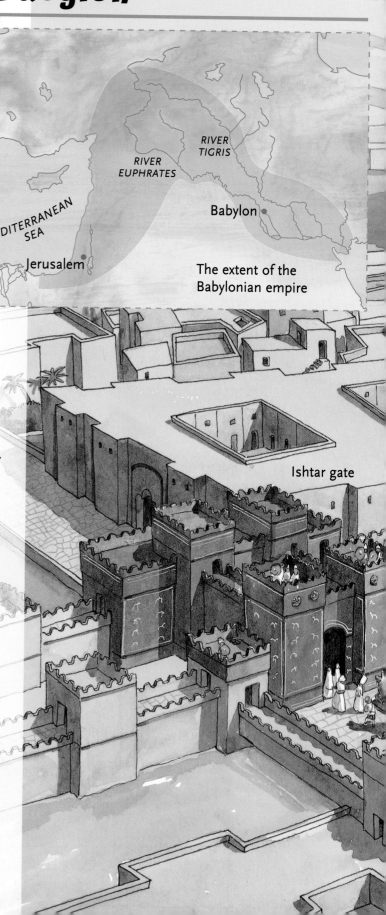

RIVER TIGRIS

RIVER EUPHRATES

MEDITERRANEAN SEA

Babylon

Jerusalem

The extent of the Babylonian empire

Ishtar gate

The fiery furnace

Once upon a time there was a king named Nebuchadnezzar. "Build me a statue," he commanded his craftworkers. "A golden statue of the god of Babylon. Set it on the plain outside the city."

Three young Jews stood and looked at the idol. "We will not bow down," they said. "We trust in our God alone."

In a city built of bricks there were plenty of furnaces. "Prepare a furnace for their execution," cried Nebuchadnezzar. "Throw those men into the flames."

Into the fire went Shadrach, Meshach, and Abednego.

But what was that? An angel came and danced in the flames and kept them safe. The king saw for himself that the God of the Jews really was the greatest God of all.

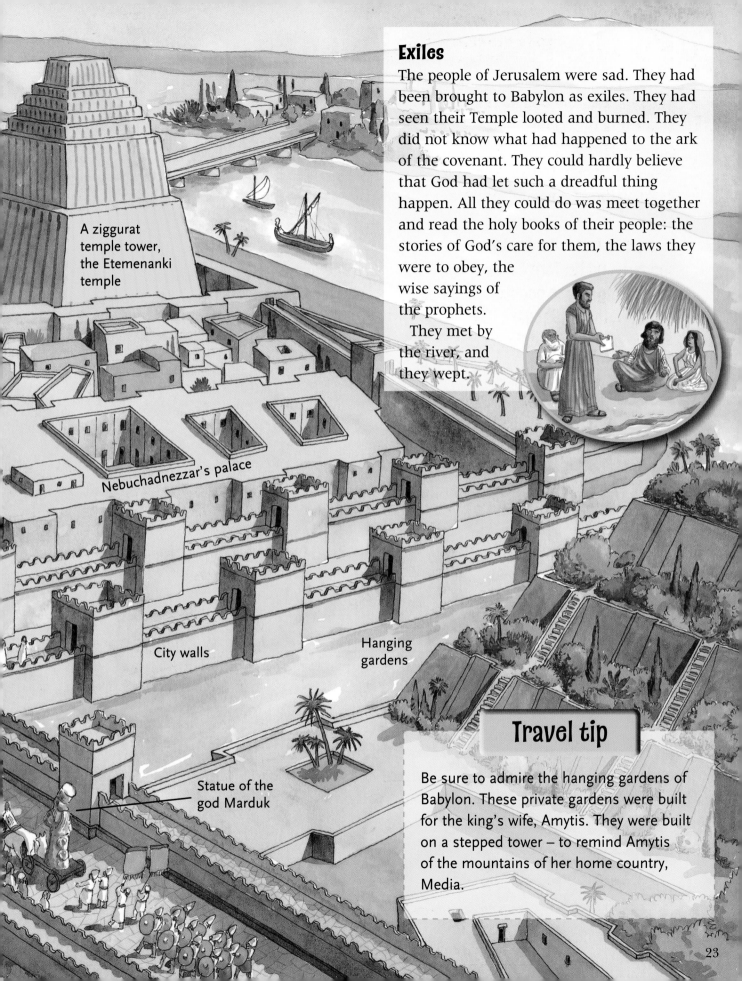

A ziggurat
temple tower,
the Etemenanki
temple

Nebuchadnezzar's palace

City walls

Hanging
gardens

Statue of the
god Marduk

Exiles

The people of Jerusalem were sad. They had been brought to Babylon as exiles. They had seen their Temple looted and burned. They did not know what had happened to the ark of the covenant. They could hardly believe that God had let such a dreadful thing happen. All they could do was meet together and read the holy books of their people: the stories of God's care for them, the laws they were to obey, the wise sayings of the prophets.

They met by the river, and they wept.

Travel tip

Be sure to admire the hanging gardens of Babylon. These private gardens were built for the king's wife, Amytis. They were built on a stepped tower – to remind Amytis of the mountains of her home country, Media.

The Persian royal court

The Babylonian empire did not last long. While the emperors enjoyed being rich and having lavish feasts, the armies of Persia were preparing to attack. They defeated Babylon and captured a huge empire of their own.

The Persian emperors knew that it was a good idea for the people they ruled to feel content. The Jews in Babylon were allowed home. Slowly they rebuilt Jerusalem and, after many years, a new Temple.

BLACK SEA

CASPIAN SEA

RIVER TIGRIS

RIVER EUPHRATES

MEDITERRANEAN SEA

Susa

Babylon

• Persepolis

Jerusalem

PERSIAN GULF

The extent of the Persian empire

Daniel and the lions

Daniel was a Jew who had been taken to Babylon at the time of the destruction of Jerusalem. He became a trusted official in the government. When the Persians came to power, the new ruler, Darius, promoted him to high rank.

At the court, enemies plotted against him. They knew that Daniel was faithful in saying his prayers. They tricked the king into punishing him for this. Daniel was thrown into a den of lions.

The king spent a sleepless night worrying about Daniel. In the morning, he hurried to the den.

By a miracle, Daniel was alive. "My God sent an angel to save me from the lions," he declared.

Travel tip

Hunting lions is a popular sport in Persia... but only for the brave and very wealthy!

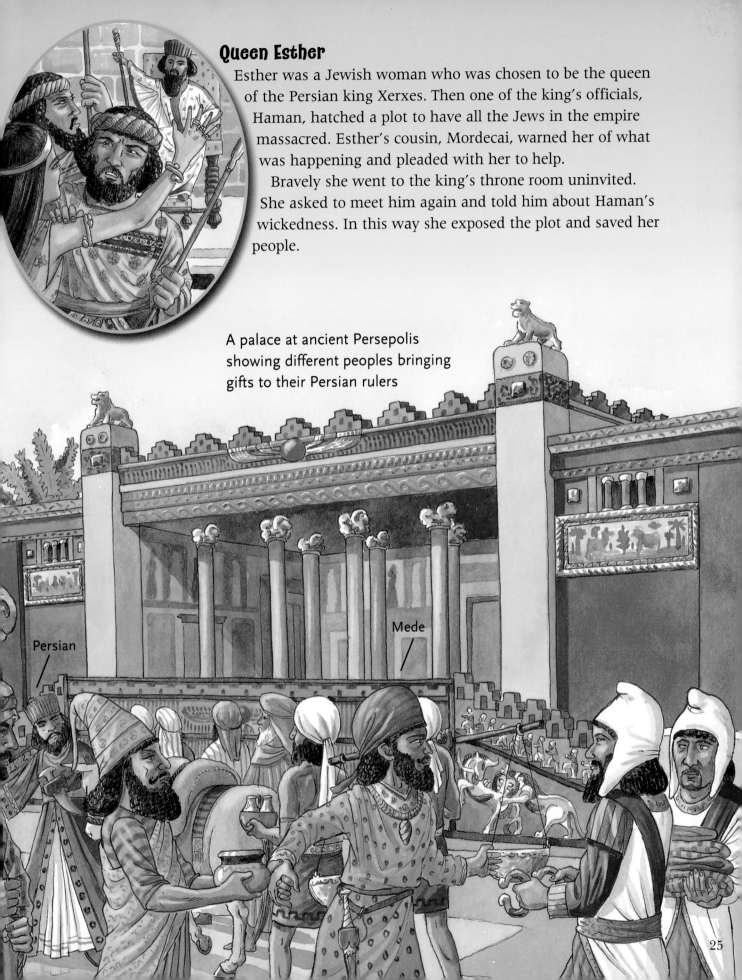

Queen Esther

Esther was a Jewish woman who was chosen to be the queen of the Persian king Xerxes. Then one of the king's officials, Haman, hatched a plot to have all the Jews in the empire massacred. Esther's cousin, Mordecai, warned her of what was happening and pleaded with her to help.

Bravely she went to the king's throne room uninvited. She asked to meet him again and told him about Haman's wickedness. In this way she exposed the plot and saved her people.

A palace at ancient Persepolis showing different peoples bringing gifts to their Persian rulers

Persian

Mede

A corner of the empire

For hundreds of years, the Jewish people were ruled by more powerful empires. First the Assyrians, Babylonians and Persians each fought for control. Then the Greeks led their armies to victory. Greek became the language of a huge empire.

The extent of the Greek empire

The books of the Jewish people do tell some stories about the time of the Greeks. The Jewish people were angry and downhearted about having to follow the Greek religion and Greek customs. Sometimes they rebelled.

Most of all, they began to pay more and more attention to the sayings of their holy people, the prophets. They had long been saying that, one day, they would have a new leader like the great kings of long ago: a king chosen by God – a "messiah".

They were still hoping for this messiah when yet another people came to power: the Romans. Their empire was bigger and more powerful than any other.

The Roman emperor chose governors to rule in different places. There came a time when the ruler of the Jewish people was a man named Herod, nicknamed "the Great". He was a cruel man but also very clever. His plan to make the Jewish people admire him was to rebuild the Temple in Jerusalem.

The Roman empire in New Testament times

ITALY

Rome

ASIA

RIVER EUPHRATES

MEDITERRANEAN SEA

EGYPT

Jerusalem

RIVER NILE

Travel tip

As with all religious buildings, pilgrims and tourists in the Jewish Temple must show respect. So-called Gentiles – anyone who isn't Jewish – may only go into the Temple courtyard. Anyone who breaks this law faces the death penalty.

The Roman garrison, the Antonia fortress

Herod's Temple

Priests offering sacrifices

High priests

Traders sell animals

Women can only go this far

Temple courtyard

The road to Bethlehem

One day, the Roman emperor Augustus gave a new order. He wanted a proper count, or census, of all the people in the empire. Then he would know how much money he could demand in taxes.

Everyone had to go to their home town to register.

It was because of this, the Bible book of Luke says, that a young couple named Joseph and Mary came from Nazareth, in Galilee, to Bethlehem. The little hilltop town was also famous as the place where King David had been born. Joseph could trace his family all the way back to David.

Roman soldiers can ask passers-by to carry their packs for a mile

Roman roads are well paved... at least some of the way

It probably took Mary and Joseph five days to walk from Nazareth to Bethlehem. They would have camped along the way

The baby in the manger

Bethlehem was crowded. Even Joseph's relations had no space left. Mary and Joseph had to make do with a stable meant for the animals. This might have been a cave. A rock-cut manger would have been a snug cradle for Mary's baby, Jesus.

That night, angels appeared to shepherds. They said that God's chosen king had been born – the messiah. They said he was cradled in a manger. The shepherds went looking and found Jesus.

The wise men

The Bible book of Matthew says that, at the time Jesus was born, some scholars who studied the night sky saw a new star. They believed it was the sign that a new king had been born to the Jewish people.

They went to the king in Jerusalem, Herod. He was angry that there might be a rival king, and wanted to kill him.

Even so, Herod's advisors were able to direct the wise men to Bethlehem, where they found Jesus.

An angel warned the wise men not to go back to Herod.

Joseph took his family to Egypt to escape Herod's anger.

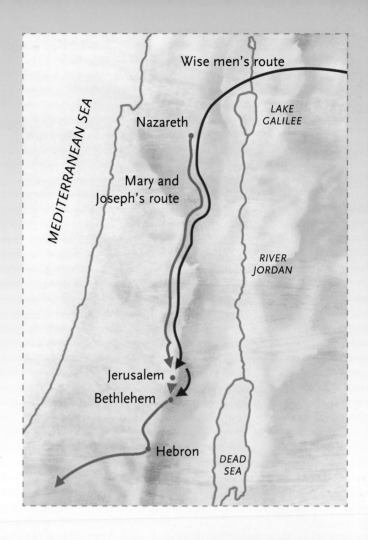

Travel tip

Most of the people who travel stay with family. Some homes will offer a room to travellers who are not family. In some cases, the "room" will be a shelter on the flat roof!

Nazareth

Joseph and Mary took Jesus to Nazareth, in Galilee. There he grew up. No one thought of him as special. To them, he was just the carpenter's son.

A carpenter's workshop

Joseph taught Jesus the skills he needed to earn his living. He would have learned to work with wood, making and mending things such as yokes for oxen, threshing sledges, and ploughs. He would also have learned about building.

Carpenters and a builder

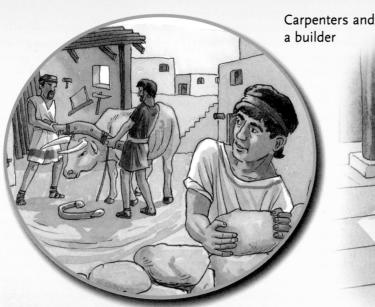

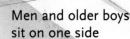

Men and older boys sit on one side

Going to school

Like all Jewish boys, Jesus would have gone to school. The teacher was called a rabbi. The boys learned to read and probably to write as well. It was important for them to be able to read from the scriptures.

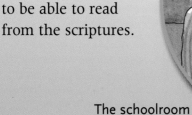

The schoolroom

The sabbath

Every week, on the sabbath day of rest, everyone met in the synagogue. Grown-up men took their turn to read from the scriptures. The rabbi explained their meaning.

The ark: the cupboard where the scriptures are kept

Scrolls on which the scriptures are written

The seven-branched lamp stand, the menorah, is a reminder of the furnishings of the tabernacle and Temple

Joseph takes his turn to read

Women and young children sit apart from the men

Travel tip

Religious teachers, or rabbis, are easy to spot. They wear leather pouches strapped to their heads. These contain words from God's Law written very small. Their shawls have extra long tassels at each corner. You may notice them on the street corner, hands held high. In this case, they are praying and they want you to walk admiringly past. If they are not praying, they like you to greet them respectfully.

31

A fishing trip from Capernaum

When Jesus was grown up, he made an important change. He became a preacher. People began to call him "Rabbi". The townsfolk of Nazareth were not impressed. "He's just the carpenter's son!" they said. They didn't want his preaching, so Jesus moved to Capernaum. This was a fishing village on the shore of Lake Galilee. Jesus became friends with some of the fishermen there.

Jesus and his fishermen friends

Four disciples

One day, Jesus was preaching by the lake shore. There were two fishing boats on the beach. Jesus got into one and asked the owner – Simon – to push it out into the water. Then the crowd came and sat on the beach. Everyone could see Jesus on the boat and hear him.

When the crowd had gone, Jesus told Simon and three other fishermen to push their boats out.

"We won't catch anything," said Simon. "We tried all last night."

Even so, they did as Jesus said and landed a huge catch.

Then they knew: Jesus was special.

"Follow me," said Jesus. "I want you to help me gather people, not fish."

They left everything to be his followers. These first disciples were Simon and his brother Andrew, James and his brother John.

Sail

Steering oars

Net

Travel tip

A boat trip on Lake Galilee is worthwhile.

Think lapping waves, a clear blue sky, the hills mauve against the skyline. However, it is very important to listen to the advice of locals about the weather. Storms can blow up without warning, and the small fishing boats quickly fill with water.

The Bible tells a story of Jesus telling a storm to stop. This event can only be classed as a miracle, and is unlikely to be repeated.

Jetty

Fish

Walking the hills of Galilee

Jesus journeyed around the hills of Galilee. Everywhere, he preached about the kingdom of God. His listeners were ordinary people and many of them wondered what he meant. Jesus told stories about their everyday world to help explain. These stories with a meaning are called parables.

Jesus welcomed children

Seeking God's kingdom

"Make it your aim to be part of God's kingdom," said Jesus. "That means doing the things God wants.

"Don't worry about food or drink. Look at the birds. They don't sow or reap, but God provides all they need.

"Don't worry about clothes. Look at the wild flowers. They don't spin or weave, but God clothes them more richly than any king."

Sheepfold

Shepherd

The sower

One day, said Jesus, a person went out to sow seeds. Some fell on the path, and birds came and ate them. Some fell on stony ground. These seeds grew, but they wilted in the sun because their roots did not go deep. Some fell among thorn bushes, and were choked by the stronger plants. Others fell on good soil and produced a harvest.

Jesus explained the parable only to his disciples.

"The seed that fell on the path means the people who hear me talk about the kingdom.

At once the Evil One comes and snatches away their understanding.

"The seed on stony ground means the people who hear the message and begin to live as part of God's kingdom. Then troubles come and they lose heart.

"The seed among the thorns means the people who hear the message and long to obey. Then everyday worries and the longing to get rich make them forget.

"The seed on good soil means the people who hear the message and obey it. They bear fruit."

The shepherd

"The way into a sheepfold is through the gate," said Jesus. "The shepherd leads the way and the sheep follow.

"I am the gate for my sheep," said Jesus. "I am the way into God's sheepfold.

"And I am the good shepherd. I am willing to die for my sheep to keep them safe. I want to gather all my sheep into one flock."

Travel tip

The hills of Galilee are at their best in spring, when the wild flowers are in bloom. The fields of blue flax are also a treat.

Wear shoes with good soles. The wild plants include many spiky plants with nasty thorns.

Plan your walk so you are back before nightfall. Not only are there jackals, foxes, and wolves; there is also a chance of meeting a leopard, a bear – or even a lion.

Ploughing

Broadcast sowing

Weeds

Stony ground

Birds

Exploring beyond Galilee

Jesus spent much of his time preaching to his own people, the Jews, in Galilee. However, he also visited other places and told people who were not Jews about God's kingdom.

The Roman officer
In Capernaum lived a Roman soldier. Jesus healed his servant by simply giving the word for this to happen.

Gadara
Near Gadara, Jesus healed a man who was troubled by what the Bible calls "evil spirits". Jesus commanded these evil spirits to leave the man alone and go into a herd of pigs. The animals ran squealing into the lake.

The Canaanite woman
Jesus once went north to the cities along the coast. A Canaanite woman pleaded with Jesus to heal her daughter, who was mentally ill. By a miracle, she was made well.

Caesarea Philippi
This place was famous as a pagan shrine. Jesus went there with his disciples and asked them, "Who do you say I am?" Simon, nicknamed Peter, replied: "You are the Christ, the Son of the living God."

Magdala
This lakeside village was the home town of Mary "Magdalene". Jesus healed her and she became a devoted follower.

Mount Hermon
On a high mountain, three of Jesus' disciples saw him "transfigured" – shining brightly as he met Moses and another great prophet. Snow-capped Mount Hermon was quite likely the place.

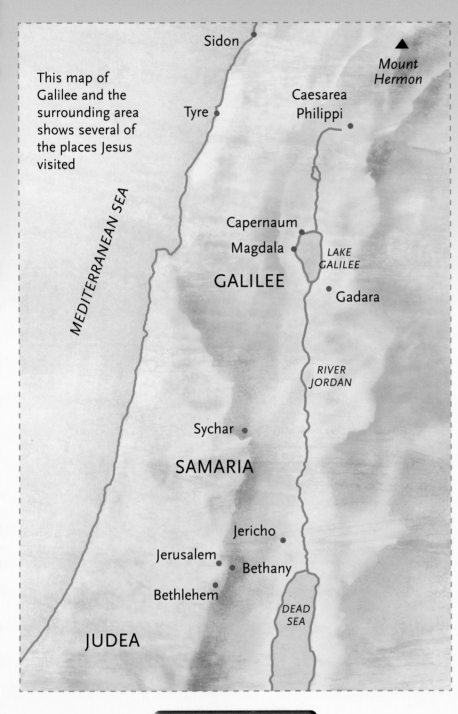

This map of Galilee and the surrounding area shows several of the places Jesus visited

Sidon

Mount Hermon

Caesarea Philippi

Tyre

MEDITERRANEAN SEA

Capernaum

Magdala

LAKE GALILEE

GALILEE

Gadara

RIVER JORDAN

Sychar

SAMARIA

Jericho

Jerusalem

Bethany

Bethlehem

DEAD SEA

JUDEA

Travel tip

It is possible to tour even the furthest places Jesus visited in a very short time. He preached in an area little more than 150 kilometres from north to south, and less than 50 kilometres from east to west. It is astonishing that his preaching has spread all round the world.

Samaria

At Sychar in Samaria, Jesus met a woman at the well. She was amazed that he, a Jew, would speak to a Samaritan. Jesus told her and her friends that the time was coming when everyone would worship God in the right way.

Jericho

In Jericho, Jesus asked to go to the house of a tax collector named Zacchaeus, who had climbed a tree to catch a glimpse of him. The townspeople were angry, because they knew Zacchaeus was a rotten cheat. However, what Jesus said to him made him mend his ways.

At home in Bethany

Bethany is a village just a few kilometres east of Jerusalem. It was the home of some good friends of Jesus: two sisters named Mary and Martha and their brother Lazarus.

The most important thing

One day, Jesus came to visit the two sisters who were his good friends. Martha hurried to get everything ready to welcome him. Mary simply sat and listened to him preaching.

Martha was suddenly angry. "Don't you care that I'm doing all the work?" she complained to Jesus. "Send her to help me."

"Poor Martha," replied Jesus. "You worry about many things, but only one thing is important. Mary has chosen to do the most important thing of all."

Well

Martha

Lazarus

Mary and Martha were both very worried. Their brother Lazarus was ill. They sent for Jesus, hoping he could heal him.

Jesus did not hurry to be with them. When he arrived, a few days later, Lazarus was dead and buried in a cave tomb.

"Don't worry," said Jesus to Martha. "I am the resurrection and the life. Those who believe in me will live, even though they die."

He asked for the tomb to be opened. He called to Lazarus – and by a miracle Lazarus came walking out.

Drying cloth

Jesus

Mary

Weaving

Travel tip

Children in a village usually entertain themselves playing simple games or watching the grown-ups at work. Your arrival will be something different and cause much excitement.

Some people find excitable children bothersome. Jesus welcomed children and said they were very important in God's kingdom.

A week in Jerusalem

Jesus' teaching was popular with many. He said that anyone who wanted to live as a friend of God was welcome in God's kingdom – even those whom others looked down on.

Many of the religious leaders were suspicious of what Jesus said. They were puzzled by his miracles and wondered how he could work them.

In the end, they plotted to get rid of him. A disciple named Judas Iscariot helped them.

Gethsema

4

1 Jesus rode a donkey into Jerusalem. Many Passover pilgrims were going to the city. A palm-waving crowd welcomed him as if he were a king.

2 Jesus went to the Temple and drove the traders out of the courtyard. "This is meant to be a place of prayer," he said. Jesus spent several days preaching in the Temple.

3 One evening, Jesus and his disciples shared a Passover meal in an upper room. One disciple, Judas Iscariot, slipped away.

4 Jesus and his disciples went to shelter for the night in an olive grove: the garden of Gethsemane. Judas led a group of soldiers there.

5 The soldiers took Jesus to the high priest's house. Jesus was put on trial in the night.

6 The next morning, on Friday, the religious leaders took Jesus to the governor, Pontius Pilate. Pilate condemned Jesus to death.

7 Soldiers took Jesus away. They whipped him and mocked him, then gave him his cross to carry.

8 The guards led Jesus carrying his cross to the place of execution: a hill outside the city named Calvary.

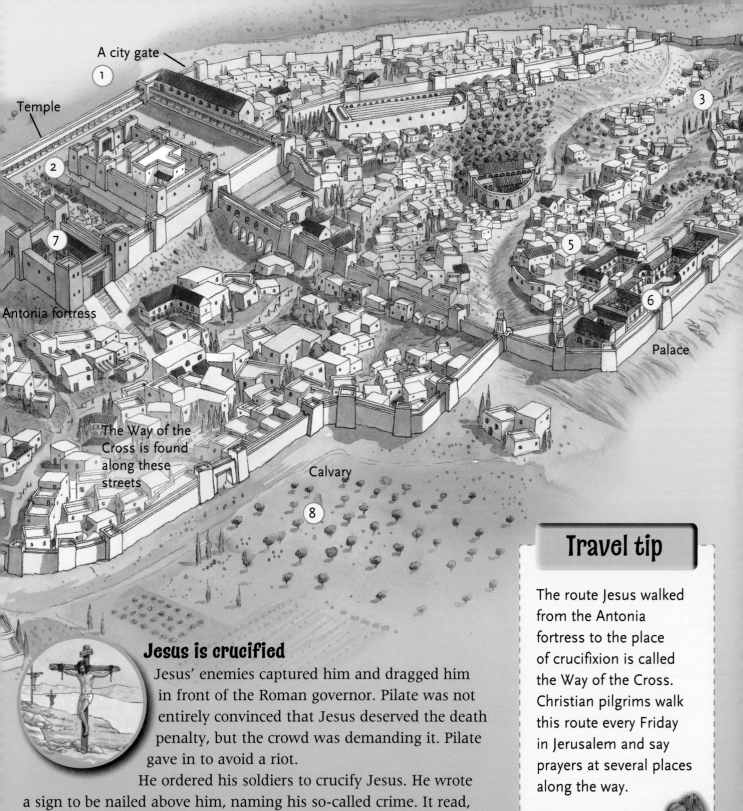

A city gate
1
Temple
2
7
Antonia fortress
3
5
6
Palace
The Way of the
Cross is found
along these
streets
Calvary
8

Jesus is crucified

Jesus' enemies captured him and dragged him in front of the Roman governor. Pilate was not entirely convinced that Jesus deserved the death penalty, but the crowd was demanding it. Pilate gave in to avoid a riot.

He ordered his soldiers to crucify Jesus. He wrote a sign to be nailed above him, naming his so-called crime. It read, "The King of the Jews".

When Jesus was dead, a follower named Joseph, who was from Arimathea, asked Pilate for permission to take the body. Joseph arranged for it to be buried in a new tomb cut in the rock. Some women who had been followers of Jesus watched as the stone door was rolled shut.

Travel tip

The route Jesus walked from the Antonia fortress to the place of crucifixion is called the Way of the Cross. Christian pilgrims walk this route every Friday in Jerusalem and say prayers at several places along the way.

News travels

The sun set on the Friday Jesus had been crucified. Next came the sabbath day of rest. Early on Sunday morning, some women went back to the tomb. One of them was Mary Magdalene.

The women found the tomb door rolled open. The body was gone. Angels told them astonishing news: Jesus was alive.

The street in Jerusalem

Jesus' disciples were afraid after the crucifixion. Soldiers might be looking for them. Certainly, it was too dangerous to appear in the city.

Then Jesus appeared to them. He told them their job was to preach the message he had preached. God would help them.

During the festival of Pentecost, they felt the power of God come over them in a gale of wind and fire. They went out into the street in Jerusalem, telling the message to pilgrims from all over the empire. Many people decided to become followers of Jesus' teaching.

Jesus' disciple Peter preaches in Jerusalem

Paul

There was a man known as Paul who disagreed strongly with what Jesus' followers preached and who tried hard to stop them. One day, he saw a bright light and heard Jesus speaking to him. The event made him change his mind. He joined the work that Jesus' disciples had begun, preaching about Jesus and his message. He preached to Jews and non-Jews alike.

In Philippi, Paul baptized a wealthy woman named Lydia, who invited believers to meet in her house

BLACK SEA

ome

PONTUS

ASIA   CAPPADOCIA

PHRYGIA   MEDIA

PAMPHYLIA

RIVER TIGRIS

PARTHIA

RIVER EUPHRATES

MESOPOTAMIA

MEDITERRANEAN SEA

ELAM

Cyrene

Jerusalem

LIBYA   EGYPT

RIVER
NILE

ARABIA

There were pilgrims from all these places in Jerusalem at Pentecost

Travel tip

At festival time in Jerusalem, you will meet pilgrims from all over the empire – and they have many different languages.

By a miracle, Jesus' disciples were able to preach in these languages on the day of Pentecost.

Anyone travelling through the empire should learn Greek. It is spoken and understood everywhere: it is the *lingua franca* of the empire.

Through the empire

Paul became a missionary for Jesus. Like many of Jesus' followers, he travelled far and wide spreading the news.

A typical port in the Roman empire

Churches

Soon there were groups of Christians in many places meeting as a church: they read the scriptures, listened to stories of Jesus, sang hymns, and said prayers. They also shared a simple meal to remember the words of Jesus to his disciples on the night before he died. He shared bread with them and said, "This is my body, broken for you." He shared wine with them and said, "This is my blood, shed for you."

Paul wrote letters to churches in these places

The journey to Rome

Paul was often in trouble for his preaching. Christianity was not a recognized religion in the Roman empire, and many people were suspicious. In the end, he asked to be sent to Rome so he could make the case about Christianity in the court of the emperor. On the way, the ship he was on was wrecked off the coast of Malta.

Paul helped keep everyone calm, and they all swam ashore.

Paul did eventually get to Rome. There he had to wait a long time for his case to be heard. He spent his time dictating letters to be taken to his friends in the churches he had set up.

The ship was destroyed by the storm, but all the passengers reached the shore safely

Travel tip

It is quite easy to travel to the newly established churches. The Roman empire has a network of roads and good shipping routes.

Index of people and places